Words to Live

Words to Live

By

Dan Semenoff

Copyright © 2015 by Dan Semenoff.

Cover photo by Dan Semenoff

Library of Congress Control Number:	2015914825
ISBN: Hardcover	978-1-5144-0548-2
Softcover	978-1-5144-0547-5
eBook	978-1-5144-0546-8

All rights reserved. No part of this book may be reproduced or transmitted in any form or by any means, electronic or mechanical, including photocopying, recording, or by any information storage and retrieval system, without permission in writing from the copyright owner.

Any people depicted in stock imagery provided by Thinkstock are models, and such images are being used for illustrative purposes only.
Certain stock imagery © Thinkstock.

Print information available on the last page.

Rev. date: 09/14/2015

To order additional copies of this book, contact:
Xlibris
1-888-795-4274
www.Xlibris.com
Orders@Xlibris.com
723686

The Forward
Furthermore
We have not even to risk
The adventure alone
For the heroes of all times
Have gone before us
The labyrinth is thoroughly known
We have only to follow
The thread of the heroes path
And where we had thought
To find an abomination
We shall find God
And where we had thought
To slay another
We shall only slay ourselves
And where we had thought
To travel outwards
We shall come to the centre
Of our own existence
And where we have thought
To be alone
We shall be
With all
The World
        As quoted
        by
        Joseph Campbell

One
Cannot choose
But
Wonder

Words
To live
By
Dan Semenoff

Be content
To be!
Find joy in it's embrace
Of simplicity.
For no love is truer
Than simple love,
Not complex or diverse,
Just there to love.
How great that feeling
And the soul knows,
Yet cannot say,
Tis enough to know,
Yet unspoken

Like a Butterfly
You land on the beach
Beside me
You spread your wings
Then fly
To another flower
A bigger rock
Always in my sight
Opening
Closing
Fluttering and
Not really showing
Seconds
I see your Beauty
Hours
Your out of sight

From daily
habits of order,
harmony,
peace and love
for these
will then
become
the automatic
expression
of your
subconscious mind
shaping your destiny
in a
positive manner

In a passage
Of time
Or in one
fleeting moment
I have
the words
then when
I gaze
and
no attention
is paid
I forgot
what
was said

There's
a man
who want to
keep you
in Hell
He's
a good man
learn from him
he'll teach
you well

High above
the mountains top
viewed
from a misty portal
myself sees
no need
for movement
the knowledge gained
is there
no need
to question
why
just sitting
watching
what goes by
up there

When children
begin to sing
it's a sign
that grownups
are doing
a good thing

        no
        matter
        how high
        or how low
        how near
        or how far
        how long
        or how short
        how good
        or how bad
        I will always
        Love You

To find to master
To love is truth
That of happiness
On a higher altitude
Truth is the doing
of undoing life
Beauty
which is truth
can make one see
even clearer
and to love
even dearer
To die of death
Is not truth
But to die of life
must be
to see my love as I do
for surly you'd love too
to embrace, to feel
is that of an Eden pasture
To crush and destroy
that of my love
would surly be
disaster

A still picture
to some
but endless
motion
of thought
to me
I'll give you
one example
"I Love You"
well
maybe
that's three

Open
your eyes
and see
the dust
flowing
within me
I've
Been shaken

                                        As
                                        I stop
                                        for a
                                        moment
                                        a sadness
                                        takes control
                                        of me
                                        the journey
                                        is over

Then
there are times
when I feel
feel
like doing things
for my self
then
there are times
when I want
want
to do more
for other

Once
I was asked
what kind
of world was I from
Once
I remembered
A kind world
I was
Still again
It will be
Again he asked
what kind
of world
are you from
and
I said
A World
I once was
And once again
I'll be

Only
within the framework
of that moment
can we appreciate
the true genius
of our brothers
Hearts
How is it
That we all feel
With the Heart
And leave it
Sealed
In a baggie

Why
Must I
Learn
I went through
evolution
and woke
as if
in Mother's arms
shocked
at Love
not knowing nor caring
a condition
for survival
why
did I
have to learn
that

But alas
We lose it all
to a hazed space
of time
gone
by that we really
can't remember
However
If we could
but capture
that fleeting moment
of insidious humor
would it matter
at all

Even
If the end
Should come
I
Would still
Stand tall

For what
I've learn't
How then
do I tell
the one
I love the most
What I feel

A little
flower
you are
to me
but
with love
and care
a Rose
you'll be

To travel
From
time
To time
Is a step
Well taken

Ah God
and the sun above
tanning
in my back yard
phone rings
she misses
me
music fades
I want to touch
seeing her face
I want to write
We laugh birds fly by
She loves
me
eyes watching
she says
pen holding tight
goodbye
I'd like to say
the words
but I think
I'll write
About the night
I loved her

If
I don't
Give
I won't
Get
If
I don't
Get
I won't
Have
If
I don't
Have
I
Won't be

Gnosis
just a thought
the world
from a horizontal
point of view
sun shinning
with ghost
in my face
the thoughts
smiling
I think yes
I want them
to work
staring
in white
I know
Thank you
head turning up
gnothi seaution
Gnosticism
just a thought

You talk to me
about my tomorrows
and you're here
to stay
I talk to you
about your today's
and you
walk away
I'm confused

                                                In Love
                                                we seek
                                                to stop
                                                the clock
                                                but
                                                find it
                                                ever ticking

Is it them
or
is it me
must be
something
I said
something
I did
I'm sorry is it them
or
is it me
nation
against nation
don't blame
me
I'm sorry
was it them
or
was it me

Son of
A father
one of
the same
I know
your Heart
Is in my brain
my love
for you
is always the same
hear me
now
know
my name

To me
I'm saying something
to you
I go on and on
to some one else
I'm just getting
started

If one
could enter
the way
he came in
and exit
the way
he left
things
would be
just peachy

Someone
I know
Is with me
I can be
but
just can't
care
no
they don't
know
confusion
In the air
Lord
I love you
Lord
I know
Your there

Man
Is a stream
whose source
is hidden
I feel
confined
every instants
to except
a greater
presence
of time
over the control
that is mine

Try not
to think
of what
others
think
you only
hurt yourself
but think
of and
for
yourself
then
they'll think
on there own
for themselves
again

So if
you'd but focus
on only
the picture
you'd but
realize
that it was
only the frame
that made
you but think
it was only
a picture

Sailing down from above
into the dimly lit room
I see your stretched face
loosely hanging on the wall
my eyes rise
from a humble bow
your face cries
the fear of pain
nailed to the cross
yet the glitter
of your blood
shines like rubies
while your tears
are faceted
like diamonds
in silence
I shriek
with an
inhaled sigh
while I stare
in amazement
and wonder
why

The thing is
that I know
the good
that is within
the thing is
to get it out

                                        Now
                                        I know
                                        how God
                                        feels
                                        when no one
                                        has faith
                                        or believes
                                        In me

Love as such
does not matter
the only thing
that does matter
is it's source
which is far
beyond
evaluation

                                      Oh
                                      what a mouth
                                        she exclaims
                                      as I say
                                      I glance
                                      in politeness
                                      to speak
                                      tis but honest
                                      and open
                                      so please
                                      pardon me

Do
what ever
you
want to do
be
who ever
you want to be
I won't change
a thing
you see
yes
I want
to know you
but all
I have
is me

I
a force
force
an energy
energy
a motion
motion
a thought
thought
a creation
creation
created self
self
a change
change
indifference
an indifference
isolation
an isolation
I
a force

All
the world
is a stage
Shakespeare
once said
and I finally
got to play
a part
in it
the fool

                                      A look
                                      into your past
                                      is a great
                                      way
                                      to see
                                      your
                                      future

To forgive
Is
Merely
To remember
Only
The loving thoughts
You gave
And those
That
Were given
You
All the rest
Must be
Forgotten

And
In return
I offer
You
A place
To rest
Within
me

Hello soul
This is
your conscious
where is your spirit
why don't
you answer
or am I
just talking
to
myself

If
I could
But do good
I
Would
But try to do better

                                          Behind
                                          every
                                          dark cloud
                                          The Son
                                          will shine

Through
the minds thoughts
and soul
through
the thoughts
of soul
and mind
through
the soul
to the thoughts
of mine

A journey
of life
is of only
one
to another
so if I stop
to smile
and say
hello
I could have
been
your brother
in one time
or another
and yet
a richer world
this would be
if you
could recognize
your face
in me

Twenty three floors
high
on a candle lit night
knowing why
the moons
filling the sky
like a bright bulbous
poking eye
below it's glow
'tis the city's
lights shinning
crushed like diamonds
in the rough
clouds rush by
and covers
it's sight
on not just
another
November
candle lit
night

I remember
on that day
that I said
I love
you
would be
the one that would break
my heart
and leave
me
on that day
I
broke my
heart
and left
you

You make it
through
awareness
older
than perception
yet born
again
in just
a moment
for what
is time
to what
was
always so ?

Think
what
that insight
brought!
oneness

It's
turning
that is
1990
I yell
out loud
the year
that is
of the horse
and I
that is
the horse
Am I

isn't it funny
that we fight
so hard
for so long
then
when it's over
and to late
do we
then see

                                              it's
                                              a hard
                                              slow
                                              climb
                                              but
                                              I've got
                                              a good
                                              heart

The next
moment
should always
be
better
than the last

　　　　　　　　　I'll act
　　　　　　　　　as though
　　　　　　　　　I am
　　　　　　　　　and
　　　　　　　　　I know
　　　　　　　　　I will
　　　　　　　　　Be

I slow
and turn
a beat
out of time
reaching
wanting
please say
yes
knees crash
ground
shakes
lighting my way
nothing
need be said
'tis done

Deception
encounters
deception
reality
itself
the meeting
of
deception
leads
to conflict
tranquility
gazing
upon itself
spreads
itself

it was
you
who taught
him
what he
knows
because
you
knew it

                                        Waiter
                                        what
                                        would you like
                                        spits
                                        in my ear
                                        music
                                        bars
                                        can't hear
                                        take your order
                                        yea
                                        beer

No two could look
on sin together
for they could
never
see it
at the same
time
strictly an individual
perception
seen in the other
yet believed
by each
to be within
himself

Brother
I have
never
been able
to talk
of love
with my fellow man
why
for I know
not what
they do
to understand
so then
their lack
of love
growth
and truth
for knowledge
is blind
how
by not searching
for the truth
within
themselves
then
we must not lose
sight
of the thought
as to what
made us blind

Within
the rain
there comes
a pain
that crashes
down
like an emotional tear
out of
it's sadness
strain
comes life
pouring fourth
from mother
nature
at her best
she grows
happiness
from
her sorrow

She arrived
at the wrong
time
yet knows
what's right
a time
to remember
a revolution
to fight
but
every time
is a wrong
time
when there's dreams
to remember
and
when it's time
to go
I'll say hello
to the highway
and kiss
the sky
for you both

We all
have dreams
that we
have to remember
like that
time
in November
when
I felt
your air
all you were saying
was
give your
dreams
a chance
to remember
the dreamer
that
I am

As to
your idea
of sin
made real
your pursuit
of being
unique
is always
at the cost
of peace
your pursuit
must
it must
give you
pain
and not
wrapped
in your
idea
to be kept
from truth again

Bodies joined
in arms
floating
face down
from above
staring
upon
the city lights
now
I have to say bye
it's dark
a blanket
over light
it was
fun
for me
I loved your joyous
nights

Please
Before you start
I would
just like to say
I think
your smart
and honest
in every way
but first
a question
I would ask of you
do you think
of what I do
is right
and while you judge
what gives you
the right
while you think
think again
I haven't
hurt you right

Will you
see
no longer
what
never was
nor
listen
to what
makes no sound

I would just
like to say
that everything
that is being said
has been said
and will be said
again

I'm still
looking
for that
great leap
forward

                                        it's getting
                                        more
                                        and more
                                        expensive
                                        to live
                                        in a
                                        free country

As he tapped
on my forehead
where my third eye
should be
He asked
the question
Well
what do you see
as I focused
for an answer
I said
I must be blind
not to see
for all I feel
is injustice
all around me
then with a glow
I began to realize
it all starts within
and around me

Dancing away
into the darkness
of stars
a distance
of a light year
give of take a
few yards
He exploded
with a glow
as in the 4th
of July
or some New Years show
three times
that second
I've witnessed
the same
his birth
his death
and his
rebirth again

the man
in the corner
doing his stuff
a boy
further down
blowing a puff
the guy
explodes
off on the stuff
knife
glaring down
my arm
stops
his try
I yell
do that
in your own mind
or
you die

*it's the one
who sponsors
the expedition
that has
the ultimate
say*

*Some times
we wonder
what's
in a mans
brain
it's practice
and
practice
again*

Walking
on water
wasn't done
In a day

Any blood shed
will be that of
citizens
but the decisions
are beyond
the information
of those
who
are actually dying

When
your truly, man
you live
in the field
of time
and know of good
on one side
and evil
on the other
live
in the center
and never
in the realization
of both terms
the
insight
transcends duality
not
the insight
of duality

When it started
it started
with a sin
in a garden of paradise
where there was
no time
men and women knew not
they were different
from each other
just like creatures
they eat the knowledge
of the pairs of opposites
covered in shame
they found
they were not the same
and God
and man are different
so it was man
and nature
against man

People
are all thinking
what
we are searching for
is a meaning for life
what we are seeking
is an experience
of being alive
life
on a physical plain
has resonance
on our inner most being
with a rapture of being alive
the mind
has to do with meaning
that which
is the experience
of life
and the inner being
of doing
the reference
transcends
all meaning

If you were
a child
you could
play
with me
like most
grown adults
wish
they could be

                                      we never
                                      really change
                                      when we
                                      become older
                                      we just
                                      become
                                      our real
                                      selves

No trace
of anything
in time
could long remain
in the minds
that serve
the timeless
and
no illusion
can disturb
the peace
of a love
that has
become
the means
of peace
and could
remembrance
of what
they are
be long delayed

as thou
art
to me
so to
I
to thee

The type
of people
you pass
every day
are very
interesting
in their own
little way

To know
that each
of us is trying
is enough
to know
each of us
cares

                                        once upon a time
                                        in a moment
                                        that once
                                        was mine
                                        you looked
                                        at me
                                        with a
                                        wonderment
                                        sigh

If I had a wish
I'd wish that I could hear
again
to hear what was right
and to know the truth
again
to hear the laughter
and know of no fight
to see your face
again
I'd know I was doing right
to feel your pain
again
if I had a wish
I'd wish
I was yours
again
tonight

Nothing comes easy
Nothing comes easy
Have I done some thing so bad
That I honestly can't remember
Nothing comes easy
Have I done some thing so wrong
That made me forget
I've lived that life
That parents taught
So well for you
To do your best
Nothing comes easy
Nothing comes easy
I grew to love them
Be honest be true
Nothing comes easy
Hurting them with words
Like I love you
Nothing comes easy
I'll bet it was some thing
That I just can't remember
or was it some thing
I was to forget
Nothing
Comes easy

Letting out my voice
every time I try
you know
it all started
with a cry
letting out my voice
like stating my opinion
cause some times
I wonder why
letting out my voice
you know
just like Mother Nature
can't you hear her
cry

T'was the night
before
Resurrection day
I thought I heard
the band
I long ago taught
to play
high on the hills
where the crosses
lay
crucifixion blues
was wailing away

Some times in my travels
I meet all kinds of people
men and women
with different traits and ideas
some wanting to control
some wanting to be controlled
and as I hear them talk
I can hear the strong
master others
but the powerful
master them selves

Life
is a good book
I always
have a laugh
as I listen
to the silence
between the lines
and I laugh
as eyebrows
are raised
when I follow
my muse

Picture a field of untouched land
with 10 inches of freshly fallen snow
that's where I'm heading
right now
to create a path
as straight as I can think it
I love straight paths
creating a path creates
a following
I like to walk the straight and narrow
a straight path is the shortest route
a path well traveled
creating a path
puts me in front
takes me to and from
it becomes well packed, well made
I've always noticed
footsteps on either side
I feel
good in knowing
I haven't walked it
alone